S0-DXM-554

SRA

READING FOR INFORMATION

Geography

People and the Environment

Mc Graw Hill **SRA**

Columbus, OH

Photo Credits

SRAonline.com

 SRA

Printed in China through Colorcraft Ltd., Hong Kong

Send all inquiries to this address:
SRA/McGraw-Hill
4400 Easton Commons
Columbus, OH 43219

ISBN: 978-0-07-610311-9
MHID: 0-07-610311-0

1 2 3 4 5 6 7 8 9 CC 13 12 11 10 09 08 07

READING for INFORMATION Geography

People and the Environment

Table of Contents

Before You Read

Here are some things you can do to help you read for information.

📖 Features Maps, Legends, and Graphs

Maps show where places are in relation to each other. Maps can show landmarks, roads, and bodies of water. The map **legend** shows what symbols on maps mean. How does the legend help you understand the map on page 27?

A **graph** can be used to support the information in a text. Look at the graph on page 18. What information does this graph show?

📝 Structures Description

Descriptions use details to help readers imagine what a place looks like. You can use a web like the one below to help you remember important details about what you read.

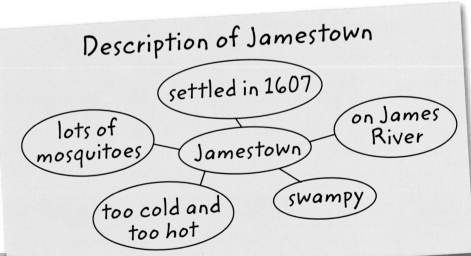

Description of Jamestown

- settled in 1607
- lots of mosquitoes
- Jamestown
- on James River
- too cold and too hot
- swampy

Vocabulary Words to Know

direction the line or course along which something moves, points, or lies

natural resource a material found in nature, such as water, that is useful to humans

population the total number of people living in an area

required to be needed

settlement the organization of people in a new country or region

site the position or location of a town, city, or building

society a community; a group set apart by some common interest or value

transportation a way of being moved from one place to another

Jamestown was the first **settlement** in the New World.

People and the Environment

New Land, New Lives

Different groups of colonists came to the New World from England in the 1600s for different reasons. They each had a plan for how to build a **society,** or community. However, the places where their ships landed largely determined how the colonists acted and what they did. The geography of the land affected their lifestyles.

The Big Question

How did the different geographies of America influence how the colonists lived?

Exploring the New World

In 1606, a group of businessmen in London, England, created the Virginia Company. Their plan was to establish a settlement. A **settlement** is an organization of people in a new country or region. These people were anxious to find gold and make their fortunes.

The three ships that crossed the Atlantic Ocean headed for a river that was known to feed into the ocean. Being on a river was important because it would provide fresh water for the settlers to drink. It could also be used for the **transportation** of goods out to the Atlantic Ocean and back to England. The river would be an easy route for ships to travel when they were bringing new supplies.

The New World c. 1763

200 Kilometers
200 Miles

Maine (part of Massachusetts)
Vermont
New Hampshire
New York
Massachusetts
Rhode Island
Connecticut
Pennsylvania
New Jersey
Delaware
Maryland
Virginia
North Carolina
South Carolina
Georgia

New England colonies
Middle colonies
Southern colonies

The Virginia Company sent the first group of English settlers to travel to the New World. What they found when they arrived was not what they expected.

Jamestown

The colonists sailed about 100 miles up the James River. They wanted to avoid conflict with settlers from Spain and France. The colonists settled in a place they named Jamestown for King James I. They named the James River after their king as well.

Jamestown seemed like an ideal **site,** or location, for the new settlement. It was almost an island, with only a sandbar connecting it to the mainland. The water was deep enough for their ships to sail right up to the land. The colonists could also defend themselves against attacks by the Spanish or Native Americans if they had to.

✓**Comprehension**

Do you think the site of Jamestown was a good choice?

This is John Smith's map of the New World from the 1600s. *How does this style of map compare to the style of map on page 7?*

Structures **Description**

What words tell you that Jamestown seemed to be a good location?

Reading for Information

Colonists soon realized Jamestown was in a poor location. *What effects did the settlement's location have on the settlers?*

The settlers soon discovered that Jamestown was a terrible location for their settlement. The land was swampy, the water was not drinkable because it was salty, and there were mosquitoes everywhere. The climate was extremely hot in the summer and bitterly cold in the winter.

The colonists got sick from diseases in the new land. They had arrived too late in the season to plant crops, so they were also low on food. Even if they had arrived earlier, they still would have struggled. Most of the colonists were businessmen, not farmers. They weren't interested in clearing land for farms. Instead, they wanted to search for gold.

The colonists continued to struggle during their first years living in the Jamestown settlement. Only 2,000 of the first 10,000 settlers in Virginia survived.

Colonists worked hard on tobacco farms. *Why did tobacco farmers need so much land to make their plantations successful?*

Plantations

The rich soil around the coast was the colonists' most valuable natural resource. This **natural resource,** or material found in nature that is useful to humans, changed how the new Virginians lived. The climate was warm, which allowed for a long growing season. There was enough rainfall throughout the year to help plants grow. The colonists discovered that tobacco grew well in this rich soil. It wasn't gold, but it soon proved to be nearly as valuable.

Growing Gold

Tobacco was very popular in England. However, it **required** a lot of land. Tobacco uses up the soil's nutrients after a few years. The soil needs to rest between growing seasons so it can replenish its nutrients. The best way for a tobacco farmer to make money was to own a lot of land. Some areas could be planted while others were resting. The more land they owned, however, the more workers tobacco farmers needed to maintain the land.

People on the Plantation

Enslaved people were brought from Africa to the colonies to help clear land and plant and harvest crops. Large tobacco farms called plantations were created in the South. All of the workers lived on the plantation. There were field workers, house servants, carpenters, blacksmiths, barrel makers, and brick makers. The plantations were like small towns.

The success of the plantations affected others in the colony. Some small farmers were pushed out of the tobacco business. There wasn't a need for small towns filled with craftspeople either, because those services could be found on the plantation. The people who owned large plantations were very wealthy. They lived in a world that resembled that of the English nobility. They dressed in fine clothes imported from England. Their furniture, silver, and linen came from England.

Some plantations had buildings for craftsmen. *What advantage did this give the plantation owners?*

Building the Southern Colonies

Groups of colonists also settled in Maryland and North Carolina, where there was more land for planting tobacco. In South Carolina, colonists discovered that the swampy land was ideal for growing rice, another crop that they could send to England and sell.

James Oglethorpe wanted to start a colony called Georgia that didn't have plantations or enslaved people. He wanted Georgia to have small farms, but the people in Georgia wanted to have big plantations. Oglethorpe ran out of money and left Georgia. Soon, the Georgians had rice plantations similar to those in South Carolina.

Rice plantations were developed across much of South Carolina and Georgia. *How did the geography of these colonies effect the success of the plantations?*

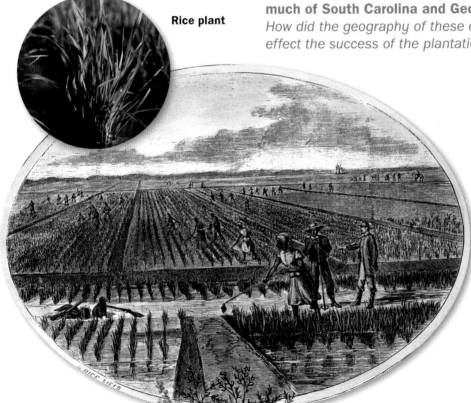

Rice plant

Reading for Information

Deerskin clothing

Life in a log cabin was quite different from life on a large plantation.

Trade Centers

Cities, such as Richmond and Baltimore, were established on waterfronts to handle the shipping of crops and other goods to England. Charleston, a city in South Carolina, had a harbor that made it easy for ships to arrive there from England. Charleston became a social center for the wealthy plantation owners and their families.

Rural Life

There were people who didn't live in a city or on a plantation. They lived away from the coast, near the foothills of mountain ranges. The land there was not as good for growing crops, such as rice or tobacco, but people could grow enough fruits and vegetables to feed their families. They built log cabins and wove their own clothes from deerskin or cloth.

The southern colonies successfully used natural resources in agriculture. The settlers in the North built a very different world.

New England

The group of colonists who became known as the Pilgrims left England for religious reasons. They wanted to be free to worship the way they wanted without interference from the Church of England. First, they settled in the Netherlands among the Dutch people. After a while, they decided to move to the New World to preserve their English culture. The Pilgrims were granted a piece of land a few miles north of the original Jamestown settlement. The plan was that they would work the land and ship goods back to England.

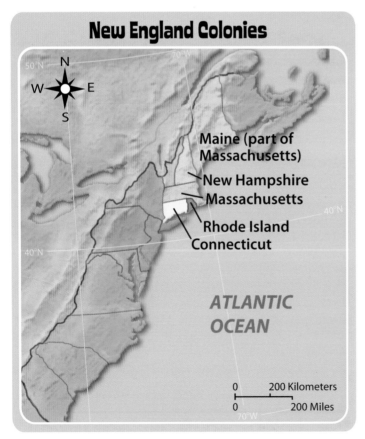

New England Colonies

Maine (part of Massachusetts)
New Hampshire
Massachusetts
Rhode Island
Connecticut

ATLANTIC OCEAN

0   200 Kilometers
0   200 Miles

Locate Virginia on the map on page 7. *Using the scale on the map above, approximately how many miles farther north is Massachusetts from Virginia?*

The Pilgrims

In 1620, a ship called the *Mayflower* set off on its journey from England to the New World. Storms threw the ship off course. The Pilgrims on the ship landed at Plymouth Harbor, which was well north of the land they had been given to settle. The colonists were exhausted from the journey. Many of them had also become sick. They didn't have the rights to the land, but they settled there and hoped for the best.

The *Mayflower*

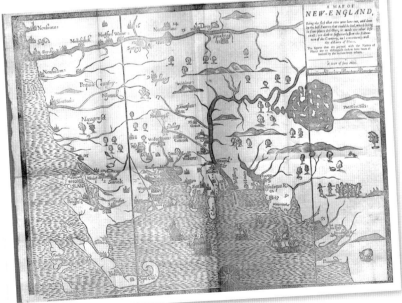

How does the map below compare to the map on page 8?

Hidden Advantages

The success of the New England colonies was due in large part to the geography of the region. New England was nothing like Virginia. The coast was very rocky, and the soil was sandy and not very rich. It was good enough for growing corn, beans, and other vegetables. However, crops such as tobacco, which was so successful in the South, would not grow in the sandy soil.

The Pilgrims often traded goods and crops with Native Americans who lived nearby. Some of the goods that were traded included corn and wheat.

New England did have some advantages. Some of the land had already been cleared for farming by Native Americans. There were some Native American tribes in the area, and the Pilgrims formed friendships with them. They began to trade with the Native Americans for food, land, and furs.

16

Learning the Land

The ocean had plenty of resources to offer. There were fish, oysters, and other shellfish for the Pilgrims to eat. The Pilgrims also saw many whales. Whales had oil that was very valuable. At first, they did not have the equipment to capture the whales. The colonists were later able to turn whaling into a big business.

The climate of New England was both good and bad for the Pilgrims. They landed in November, when it was snowy and cold. These conditions helped the Pilgrims avoid some of the diseases that killed the colonists in the swampy, mosquito-infested Jamestown. However, because the winter was so harsh, about half of the *Mayflower*'s passengers did not survive the first year. Illness, cold weather, and poor nutrition killed 52 of the first 102 settlers. The rest were able to build a settlement.

✓**Comprehension**
How do you think the colonists prepared for the cold winters?

Colonists often fished in the rivers and streams in New England. The ocean was another important natural resource for them.

The Economy of the North

The location of the harbors in New England made it easy for ships to come and go. The **population,** or total number of people living in an area, grew as colonists settled in other parts of New England. They moved to western Massachusetts, Connecticut, New Hampshire, Rhode Island, and Maine.

Towns used streams to power mills. These areas would later become centers for factories and manufacturing.

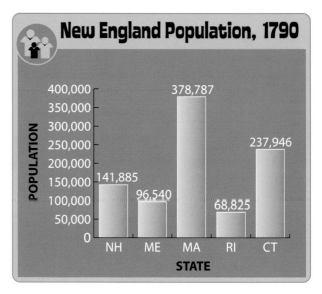

New England Population, 1790

Why do you think Massachusetts had the largest population?

The colonists fished for cod and sold it to England. They built ships and sent logs from the trees back to England. They farmed and raised sheep, goats, and cows that were brought over from England.

Small towns were established everywhere. Each town centered around a meetinghouse that served as both the church and town hall. Craftsmen, who made furniture, silver, soap, and candles, settled close to the meetinghouses.

Reading for Information

Different Lives, Same Continent

The people of New England had different lives from the people of the southern colonies. Some rich people had enslaved people who worked in their houses. However, enslaved people were not as important to New England as they were in the South. The busy seaport cities and fishing towns of New England were far different from elegant southern cities such as Charleston and Savannah. Although there were wealthy people in New England, many of them had religious beliefs that encouraged simplicity.

Like the Virginians, the people of New England recreated a little piece of England. However, they copied the culture of small English towns, not the wealthy manor houses and estates. Life in the two regions was very different.

The red house is in New England. The plantation house is in the South. *How would you describe the differences between these images?*

genre Travelogue

A travelogue gives information about a person's visit to a new location. Travelogues are important because they provide descriptions about areas of the world. The pieces below are fictional accounts of visits to Boston in two different centuries.

BOSTON, 1638

When I walk along the shore, my eyes are constantly amazed by the richness of the sea. We have pulled clams out of the mud with our bare hands, and one can barely take a step without hearing the crack of an oyster shell. The stream behind our house is so filled with fish that I think I could walk across the water on their backs.

The land is equally astounding. There are many types of birds—cardinals, jays, doves, crows, and, of course, ducks and geese. We have found a lot of sweet berries in the forest. It is much different from London.

Colonial Boston

N

Charles River

Beacon Hill

Boston Common

Newberry Street

Boston Harbor

BOSTON, 2008

We have been very busy since we arrived in Boston. The traffic is crazy, and finding a parking spot is almost impossible. However, there are so many great things here. We've seen buildings that are hundreds of years old, and we've walked along streets that were built by the first settlers. It's almost like stepping into the past!

We have eaten at many different restaurants. We also visited Quincy Market where Bostonians have been shopping for over 200 years. We're going to a Red Sox game tonight, and then we're off to Cape Cod tomorrow. I can't wait to lie on the beach and listen to the waves!

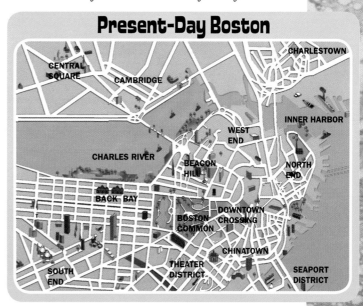

Present-Day Boston

CHARLESTOWN

CENTRAL SQUARE

CAMBRIDGE

INNER HARBOR

WEST END

CHARLES RIVER

BEACON HILL

NORTH END

BACK BAY

DOWNTOWN CROSSING

BOSTON COMMON

CHINATOWN

THEATER DISTRICT

SOUTH END

SEAPORT DISTRICT

The Middle Colonies

In 1664, the English took over the Dutch colony of New Netherland. The new colony had mountain ranges, deep valleys, farmland, and thousands of lakes and streams. The Hudson River flowed from the harbor on the Atlantic Ocean all the way to the mountains in the northern part of the colony. The river was useful for shipping goods.

The Dutch had many other colonies around the world, so they did not mind giving this colony to the English. The new owners of the colony changed the Dutch names to English names. They gained land that is now New York State, Delaware, and New Jersey.

Which colony is north of Pennsylvania?

✓**Comprehension**
In what other ways do you predict the colonists used the Hudson River?

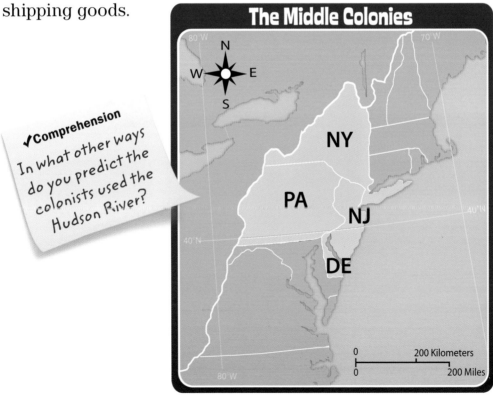

The Middle Colonies

Reading for Information

New Amsterdam

The Dutch had invited people from Norway, Sweden, Germany, and Denmark to their colony. By 1660, there were about 1,000 people living in New Amsterdam, a busy Dutch port city on what is now the island of Manhattan.

The English didn't ask the Dutch and other colonists to leave. The colony was doing well. The harbor and Manhattan Island were busy with ships. The other islands in the area, today's Long Island and Staten Island, had excellent land for farming. Businessmen even formed a stock market in Manhattan. Business was good in New York.

Colonial family

Manhattan Island was settled by people from many different countries.

Pennsylvania

Another colony that was founded for religious reasons was Pennsylvania. William Penn, a wealthy English Quaker, wanted to start a colony where people could live and practice their religions safely. To pay off a debt, King Charles II gave Penn the land to start the colony.

Philadelphia

Penn wanted to create an important city for his colony. He chose a spot where the Delaware and Schuylkill rivers meet so ships could easily travel up and down the rivers and out to the Atlantic Ocean. This city, named Philadelphia, became a center of trade.

Philadelphia had wide streets, and the lots for the houses were spacious. The streets were paved with bricks made from the red clay found along the riverbanks. Many of the houses were also made from brick. Philadelphia was considered one of the New World's most beautiful cities.

The bricks used to build Philadelphia can still be found in certain areas of the city.

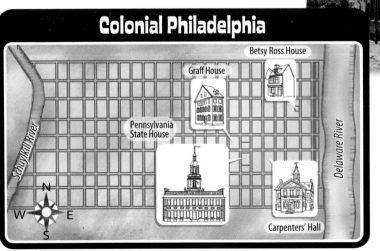

Colonial Philadelphia

Betsy Ross House

Graff House

Pennsylvania State House

Schuylkill River

Delaware River

N
W   E
S

Carpenters' Hall

Reading for Information

Philadelphia was also a profitable city. Like Boston, people there were heavily involved in shipping and shipbuilding. Many craftsmen had businesses in the city. Some colonists moved out to the countryside where there was rich soil for farming and grasslands for raising dairy cows. By the middle of the 1700s, coal and other minerals were found in the hills of Pennsylvania.

A Natural Blend

The Middle Colonies of New York, New Jersey, Delaware, and Pennsylvania were founded for both religious and business reasons. The coastlines and rivers allowed colonists in the region to build important port cities. The Middle Colonies also had plenty of countryside where people could farm. With both farms and port towns and cities, the Middle Colonies represented a blend of the agricultural South and business-centered North.

Pennsylvania still has a lot of countryside.

Coal is an important natural resource found in the hills of Pennsylvania.

Environmental Effects

The colonization of the New World had a huge impact on the environment. As the colonists used what they needed to build their new civilization, they changed the land forever.

Deforestation

Forests were chopped down as the colonists cleared land for their farms. They used the wood from the trees to build their houses. Wood was used in fireplaces for heat and cooking too. Colonists also shipped wood to England, where it was used as building material.

The loss of forests made the soil warmer and drier. In some areas, the soil dried up. In other areas, the soil did not drain enough, turning the land into permanent swamps. Animals also lost their habitats and had to find new homes.

✓Comprehension
What effect do you think settlers had on the land?

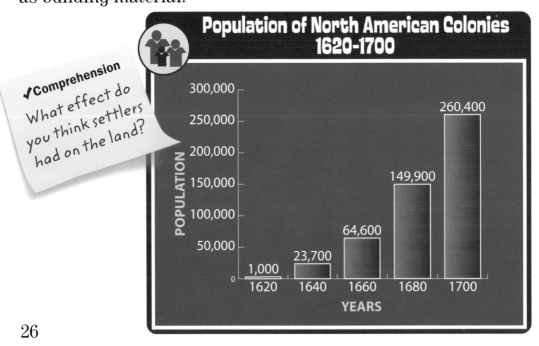

Population of North American Colonies 1620-1700

26

Soil and Water

Soil was affected by farming. Tobacco and corn were hard on the soil. The Native Americans had grown a lot of corn, but they moved from place to place each year. The colonists, however, wanted to settle in one place. They wore out the soil by planting the same crops over and over again in the same place.

Fishing was a big business in New England. Over the years, the colonists fished some species until they nearly became extinct. When one species disappeared or moved, larger fish also lost them as a food source. Each change in the land or water caused the colonists to seek out new food sources.

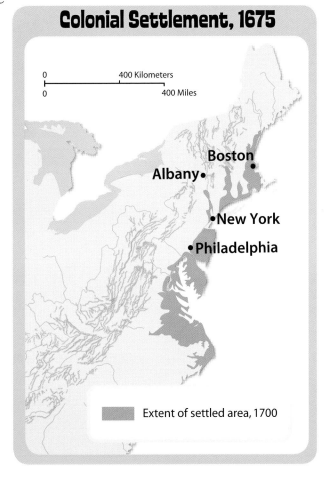

Colonial Settlement, 1675

0   400 Kilometers

0   400 Miles

Boston

Albany•

•New York

•Philadelphia

Extent of settled area, 1700

Overcoming Obstacles

When the colonists arrived, there seemed to be a limitless supply of natural resources. The forests looked like they went on forever and the water appeared to contain thousands upon thousands of fish. The possibility of using up any of these resources probably did not even occur to the early colonists.

Some of the new land provided obstacles for the Americans. As they continued moving west, they found mountains, deserts, and flat plains. Each group of settlers in these areas had to adjust their lifestyles so that they could work with the land. The different landscapes of the country affected its development. Each area formed distinct economies, and the people had varying lifestyles.

The geography of the colonies was as diverse as the people. There were seacoasts, lush forests, and acres of farmland.

Geographical Impacts

Each place the colonists landed provided some type of resource. Whether it was good land for farming, forests for hunting and cutting down wood, or the water for fishing and trade, geography played a major role in how each colony developed.

Think about your community. Are there parks where homes can't be built? Some of these parks are homes for wildlife who have lost their habitats as Americans have used up their land. Are there new buildings or homes being built near you? Many trees may have been cut down to clear the land. If you live near water, you may notice signs that prohibit fishing. This is to protect the marine life so that it does not become extinct. How the colonists used the land years ago directly impacts your life today.

Today, some forests have signs to explain that they are protected from future development.

Think about It! How do you think the geography of where you live impacts your daily life?

Complete these activities on a separate piece of paper.

ABc Vocabulary Words to Know

Choose the sentence in which the underlined vocabulary word is used correctly.

1. **a.** The eye doctor told me I had excellent <u>site.</u>

   b. We chose a <u>site</u> for our picnic.

2. **a.** Horses were a form of <u>transportation.</u>

   b. The colonists used chickens and pigs for <u>transportation.</u>

3. **a.** Gold is a <u>natural resource.</u>

   b. Clothes are a <u>natural resource.</u>

4. **a.** The colonists cleared a field to plant a rice <u>settlement.</u>

   b. Jamestown was the first permanent British <u>settlement</u> in North America.

5. **a.** The <u>population</u> of our town grows every summer.

   b. My aunt live on a beautiful <u>population.</u>

Features Maps, Legends, and Graphs

Use the map on page 24 to answer Question 6.

6. Which river is east of Philadelphia?

Use the graph on page 18 to answer Question 7.

7. How many people lived in Rhode Island in 1790?

 **Structures** **Description**

Use the information about New York on page 22 to answer Question 8.

8. What are some of the descriptive words the writer uses to help you picture what New York looked like?

Write about It

Write about how the geography where you live has affected who you. Describe how the area in which you live affects the weather, the types of activities you participate in, how you travel, and what types of jobs are available in your area.

 Go To

Interactive Skills Handbook

For more practice with

➡ **predicting,** see pages 90–93.

➡ **description,** see pages 58–65.

➡ **maps and legends,** see pages 34–37.

➡ **graphs,** see pages 18–21.

Glossary

direction (di rek' shən) *n.* the line or course along which something moves, points, or lies. *I changed my direction and went south instead.*

natural resource (nach' ər əl rē sôrs) *n.* a material found in nature that is useful to humans. *Water is an important natural resource.*

population (pop' yə lā shən) *n.* the total number of people living in an area. *The population of our town was 12,298 last year.*

required (ri kwīrd') *v.* to be needed. *The new law required us to wear bicycle helmets.*

settlement (set' əl mənt) *n.* the organization of people in a new country or region. *The first people to arrive in the settlement cleared land and built houses.*

site (sīt') *n.* the position or location of a town, city, or building. *The colonists built on a site near the river.*

society (sə sī' i tē) *n.* a community; a group set apart by some common interest or value. *Quakers were a religious society.*

transportation (trans por tā shən) *n.* a way of being moved from one place to another. *My bicycle is my favorite form of transportation.*

Pronunciation Key

a	at	**i**	it	**ou**	out	**ch**	chair
ā	late	**ī**	kite	**u**	up	**hw**	which
ä	father, ox, mop	**ō**	rose	**ū**	use, mule	**ng**	ring
âr	care	**ô**	law, bought	**ûr**	turn, learn	**sh**	shop
e	set,	**oi**	coin	**ə**	about,	**th**	thin
ē	me	**o͞o**	book, pull		chicken,	**t͟h**	there
ē	me	**o͞o**	food, rude		pencil,	**zh**	treasure
îr	ear, pier	**or**	form		cannon,		
					circus		